MAKE $150,000 A YEAR AT FESTIVALS

MAKE $150,000 A YEAR AT FESTIVALS

BY

Jeanne Storeim

PRIMIX
PUBLISHING
THE WRITE CHOICE

Primix Publishing
East Brunswick Office Evolution
1 Tower Center Boulevard, Ste 1510
East Brunswick, NJ 08816
www.primixpublishing.com
Phone: 1-800-538-5788

Published by Primix Publishing: 03/24/2025

ISBN: 979-8-89194-458-9(sc)
ISBN: 979-8-89194-459-6(e)

Library of Congress Control Number: Pending

CONTENTS

Chapter 1. Things You Need
to Know 1

Chapter 2. Juried? 5

Chapter 3. Finding the Best
Shows 10

Chapter 4. Planning a Calendar 19

Chapter 5. Applying to Events. . 23

Conclusion 27

CHAPTER 1

Things You Need to Know

If you have decided you want to sell things at fairs and festivals you will be pleasantly surprised at the number of events that are available to you. The variety is quite large so I am going to give you information that will help you find the best fit for you and your products.

There are different categories of events and it is important that you know the difference so you don't waste your time and money applying to events that are not designed for your product.

"ART SHOWS"

"ART" is defined as a product that is more focused on using tools and materials to express an emotion or idea.

"CRAFT SHOWS"

"CRAFTS" is more focused on using tools and materials to create a specific object or product. They are generally products that can be used or have a specific purpose.

FESTIVALS

Festivals are open to a bigger variety of vendors and often draw larger crowds because they offer food and entertainment.

When you go to an art fair you can expect to see paintings, sculptures, blown glass, metal worked jewelry, photography, and more along those lines.

At craft fairs you will see handmade items like soap, embroidery, candles, jellies and jams, and other handmade items.

These are just a few of the multitude of items you will see, but it gives you a broad overview.

Festivals are a little different. Festivals accept applications for art, craft, retail and services such as travel programs and home improvement products. The application for this type of event isn't limited by the type of product you have.

CHAPTER 2

Juried?

A juried event is where vendors present their products to be juried against other applicants. A non-juried event allows vendors to apply with no evaluation of their work, product or art.

A jury typically consists of people who have some level of experience in the arts and crafts industry. They assess applicants work based on quality, uniqueness, and presentation.

The level of product scrutiny in the jury process is extremely broad. If you are applying to a juried event that is very popular, the competition can be quite fierce.

If you are applying to a small craft show, the process may be little more than a formality to avoid over duplication of the same type of product.

The experience of jurors varies widely.

EXAMPLE

If applying to an art show put on by the art league these jurors are involved in the art world and usually have a pretty good base of knowledge in that area.

Smaller craft fairs and festivals are usually pretty open about accepting any product into the event.

The best way to get a feel for whether an event is a good fit for you is to read the application carefully. Often they will clearly state what is and is not accepted.

Another great way to evaluate a show is to look at their website of past years events. Look at the booth pictures and the products that were there. Does it look like the type of items that fit well with your product? Also look at the pictures of people attending the event. Do they look like the segment of the population that is interested in your product?

EXAMPLE

You see pictures of wooden toys, candles and jams and the crowd is comprised of mostly young couples with children. This may be a good match is you sell inexpensive items but may not be a good match if you sell high end art.

CHAPTER 3

Finding the Best Shows

There are a number of ways you can find events to sell your products. Let me break this down into specific sites to give you a concrete starting place.

Festivalnet.com is one of the sites that offers not only nation- wide listings but also offers some of the most useful detailed information available anywhere. You can access the site free of charge and will be able to see events in every state.

Using this site you can select events by location and date. Given this information you can do a google search for the event website.

Other sites that offer similar information are:

Fairs and Festivals
Festival Guides and Reviews
Where the Shows Are
Zapplication
Eventeny

Some of these sites offer additional information with a membership fee.

Now that you know to use the location and date let's fine- tune your search. Festivalnet offers a paid subscription that gives you much more detailed information on each event and also an online store site for you to sell your products. The annual subscription fee is very reasonable and if you use the information you will definitely get your money's worth.

Using your Festivalnet privileges you can select your event by state or distance from your zip code, juried or not juried, music and more qualifiers.

For each event it also lists:
Promoter name
Other events by this promoter
Name of person in charge
Phone #
Email
Deadline to apply
Link to website

You can click to go directly to the website to see pictures of previous years events to see if it looks like a good match. You can also usually access the application from the website.

The contact information is extremely helpful especially if you have any questions.

Other information that is important is the number of people attending the event. This lets you know how many prospective customers you will be exposed to. It also lists the number of vendors. These are two of the most important pieces of information you use to determine which events are better for you.

If a show is small (has a small number of people attending and a small number of vendors) a larger % of the people will purchase your product because there a limited number of vendors. This is a larger %, not number of sales.

At larger events, you are exposed to a much larger number of potential buyers but will get a smaller % of purchase dollars because you have more vendors. Generally, larger shows produce much more dollar volume even though the % is smaller.

As you can see, the information you have should go a long way in helping you decide which event will work the best for you.

Here is an example of how you can estimate income from events. These are just hypothetical figures, but the formula is based on fact.

Based on
% of attendees who purchase your product
%1-%5
Average price of product
$20
(this is a very conservative estimate)

SMALL SHOW

1000 attendees   25 vendors   5%
1000 x 5% x $20 = $1000

MEDIUM SHOW

30,000 attendees   100
vendors   1%
30,000x 1% x $20=$6000

LARGE SHOW

50,000 attendees   200
vendors   1%
50,000 x 1% x $20=$10,000

If you are willing to commit to being a vendor at events on a full -time basis, $150,000 per year is a reasonable income expectation. If you make $3000 per weekend and do 50 events per year you have reached this income point. There are a number of variables that are going to move that number but, a lot of them can propel you significantly past $150,000.

CHAPTER 4

Planning a Calendar

If you are contemplating doing events regularly you may want to create a calendar to keep track of events you are interested in, have applied to, and where you have been accepted into an event.

On your calendar select the dates you would like to fill and list the events that interest you.

EXAMPLE:

Craft Show   Your Hometown
1000 attendees   25vendors   I day
Pros= no travel expense -any
product
Cons= low attendance-only one day

Art Show   Close to Hometown
30,000 attendees   100 vendors   2
days
Pros- no travel expense- full
weekend show
Cons-Products must be art

Large Festival

50,000 attendees   200 vendors
3 days
Pros- any product- 3- day event
Cons-Travel expense

Eliminate the shows that don't seem like a good fit. For example, you may have a product that doesn't fit the show or you may not want to do a three- day event. You can go back to the listing sites and look at more options. You can expand your search area or go to a different event listing site. The event listings may overlap but, they all have different events.

Once you have a list of events that look interesting use the information you have to weed out the least appealing and do the same calculations like the example to get a better feel for which event would be best for you.

CHAPTER 5

Applying to Events

Now that you have chosen an event, you are going to apply to be a vendor. Every event has its own application and some are longer than others and want more information. If you prepare ahead of time the application process can go pretty quickly.

Here is a list of things you should have ready to start filling in the application:

Your company name
Your name
Email
Phone
Mailing address
Product medium
Pictures of product
Pictures of booth

Product medium is just a categorization of the types of products sold at events. Art shows are more likely to want a product designation but, other shows use it as well. Often so they can control the number of vendors in each category. The application will usually have a list of categories to choose from.

Most events want a booth or display picture and multiple product pictures. If you take the time to produce quality pictures of your product and an inviting look to your display you have a much better chance of being accepted into an event.

When looking at events, note the dead-line for getting your application in. Some events fill in spaces on a first come basis so get your application in early.

CONCLUSION

You now have a lot of information to help you find events and to decide which ones will work for you. I hope this has helped you get started on a path that gives you a great deal of financial success and lets you design a lifestyle you thoroughly enjoy.

Jeanne Storeim